Read All About Whales

WHALES OF THE SEAS

Jason Cooper

The Rourke Corporation, Inc.
Vero Beach, Florida 32964

PHOTO CREDITS
©James D. Watt/INNERSPACE VISIONS: p.4; ©Lynn M. Stone: p.6,10, 20; ©Marty Snyderman: p.7,18; ©Tom Campbell: p.15; ©Brandon Cole: p.16; ©Peter C. Howorth: p.9,12,19; ©1996 Sea World of Florida, All Rights Reserved: p.13; ©Tom Kitchin: cover, p.22

Library of Congress Cataloging-in-Publication Data

Cooper, Jason, 1942-
   Whales of the seas / by Jason Cooper
      p. cm. — (Read all about whales)
   Includes index.
   Summary: Describes the habitat, physical characteristics, life cycle, behavior and different kinds of whales.
   ISBN 0-86593-453-3
   1. Whales—Juvenile literature. [1. Whales.]
I. Title II. Series: Cooper, Jason, 1942- Read all about whales
QL737.C4C654 1996
599.5—dc20
                                96–19193
                                     CIP
                                       AC

Printed in the USA

TABLE OF CONTENTS

Whales of the Seas .5

Cetaceans 6

Kinds of Whales .8

Teeth and Baleen 11

Baby Whales 12

Whale Pods 14

Flippers and Flukes 17

Blubber 18

Whale Breath 20

Glossary 23

Index 24

WHALES OF THE SEAS

Whales and their smaller cousins, the porpoises and dolphins, look much like fish. They live in the seas like fish and swim like fish.

Whales, though, are **mammals** (MAM uhlz), like people. Whales breathe air and they are warm-blooded. Baby whales grow up on their mother's milk, like other mammals.

Whales aren't covered with hair or fur, as most other mammals are. They do, however, have a few stiff hairs on otherwise smooth bodies.

Whales live in the seas, but they are air-breathing mammals, like people.

CETACEANS

Scientists call porpoises, dolphins, and whales **cetaceans** (seh TAY shunz). Cetaceans—the whale family members—are special mammals. They spend their entire lives in the water.

Like cetaceans, manatees are mammals with two front flippers. They eat plants.

Cetaceans are the porpoises, dolphins, and great whales, like the humpback shown here.

The only other mammals living full time in the water are **sirens** (SI rehnz). The **manatee** (MAN uh TEE) of Florida and the West Indies is the only North American siren.

Cetaceans eat animals while sirens are plant eaters. Nearly all cetaceans live in the sea. Sirens live in rivers and shallow saltwater bays.

KINDS OF WHALES

Scientists divide the whale family into two major groups, the **baleen** (buh LEEN) whales and the toothed whales.

Most of the 10 species, or kinds, of baleen whales are huge. One of them, the blue whale, is the largest animal on Earth. Blue whales reach 100 feet in length.

The 66 species of toothed whales are generally smaller. The toothed group included porpoises, dolphins, and one truly great whale, the 60-foot sperm whale.

A giant blue whale, one of the baleen whales, cruises in the company of a cousin, the common dolphin.

TEETH AND BALEEN

Baleen whales are toothless. They trap food in overlapping plates of baleen that hang from their upper jaws. Baleen, like your fingernails, is made of **keratin** (KER uh tin). Baleen is tough, but lightweight.

Killer whales and other toothed whales catch prey with their teeth. Toothed whales eat mostly fish and squid. Baleen whales eat small fish and tiny, floating creatures called **plankton** (PLANK ton).

A section of blue whale baleen shows the bristlelike edges that trap plankton.

BABY WHALES

A female, or cow, whale normally has just one baby at a time. The baby, or calf, is born underwater. The mother must push it immediately to the surface for its first breath.

A mother protects her newborn for at least a year. Some whales travel with their mothers and other family members for several years.

A common dolphin with her calf skips over the waves.

A young killer whale seems to enjoy the attention of its trainer and a new friend.

Young whales grow quickly on mother's milk rich in fat. Baby blue whales gain 200 pounds a day on it!

WHALE PODS

Whales of all kinds have many of the same habits and body features. For example, whales great and small have streamlined, fishlike shapes. Almost all whales are social, too. They like each other's company.

Whales travel in groups called schools, or pods. Some pods have several hundred members at certain times of the year.

By traveling in groups, whales have more eyes and ears alert for prey and predators.

Bottle-nosed dolphins (shown here) and other cetaceans usually travel in pods.

FLIPPERS AND FLUKES

The whale's front "legs" are actually paddle-shaped flippers. Flippers are much more useful for a **marine** (muh REEN), or ocean, animal than a leg like yours would be. The bones in a whale's flippers, though, are similar to other mammals.

A whale steers and keeps its balance by using its flippers. A whale moves by flexing its flukes, or tail, up and down.

A leaping humpback whale shows off its extremely long flippers.

BLUBBER

Whales don't have hair for warmth. They have a layer of blubber, or fat. Blubber keeps whales warm, and it's a whale's food pantry. When a whale travels and food is scarce, it can live off its blubber.

Right whales have the thickest blubber of big whales. These whales were easily hunted and killed, so whalers called them the "right" whales.

Big whales, like the blue in this photo, can live on the energy stored in their blubber.

The thickness of blubber depends upon the kind of whale. The big right whale has a 20-inch coat of blubber. Other large whales have blubber just six inches thick.

WHALE BREATH

Whales, like people, breathe air through their lungs. Whales must swim to the ocean surface to breathe.

Baleen whales usually surface for air every 5 to 15 minutes. Some, however, can stay undersea for an hour if they must.

Whales breathe through openings in their heads known as blowholes. When a whale breathes air out, it sends up a spout, or blow, of mist. When a whale dives, it closes the blowhole.

The blowhole on the top of a toothed whale's head (shown here) has a single opening. Baleen whales have twin openings.

GLOSSARY

baleen (buh LEEN) — the tough, comblike plates found in the upper jaws of certain whales; whalebone

cetacean (seh TAY shun) — the group of marine mammals with two flippers and animal food diets; the whales, porpoises, and dolphins

keratin (KER uh tin) — the tough material of which both whale baleen and human fingernails are made

mammals (MAM uhlz) — the group of air-breathing, warm-blooded, milk producing animals

manatee (MAN uh TEE) — a plant eating marine mammal of the siren family

marine (muh REEN) — of or relating to the ocean

plankton (PLANK ton) — tiny, floating plants and animals of the sea and other bodies of water

siren (SI rehn) — a small family of marine mammals that eat plants and live in seas and coastal rivers

A killer whale blows at sunset along the British Columbia coast in Canada.

INDEX

baleen   8, 11

blowhole   20

blubber   18

cetaceans   6

dolphins   5, 6, 8

flippers   17

flukes   17

keratin   11

mammals   5

manatees 6

milk   13

plankton   11

pods   14

porpoises   5, 6, 8

whales   5, 6, 8, 12, 14, 18, 20

  baby   13

  baleen   8, 11, 20

  blue   8, 13

  killer   11

  right   18

  sperm   8

  toothed   8, 11